The *boundless* Energy of the Heart
of the

Children don't just need to be loved;
they need to know that nothing they do
will change the fact that they are loved.

- Alfie Kohn -

A catalogue record for this book is available from the National Library of Australia

Kodra, Rovena (author)
The Boundless Energy of the Heart:
Are you giving your child the best version of you?

ISBN 978-1-922337-38-2

EDUCATION / Parent Participation
FAMILY & RELATIONSHIPS / Parenting / Motherhood
FAMILY & RELATIONSHIPS / Parenting / General

Typeset Whitman 11/12

Cover and book design by Green Hill Publishing

Contents

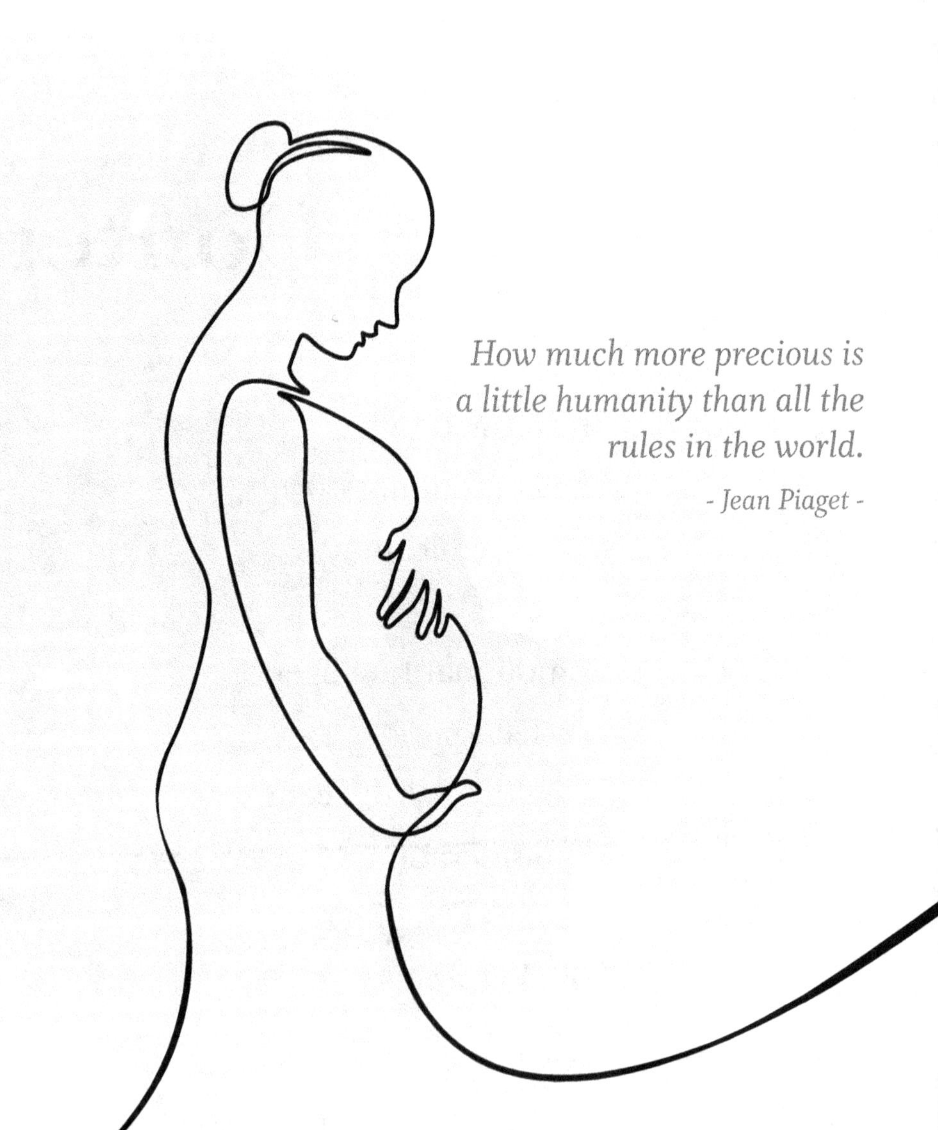

*How much more precious is
a little humanity than all the
rules in the world.*

- Jean Piaget -

Introduction

This book was not written to tell parents how they should or shouldn't raise their children, because no one knows your child better than you do. This book is an invitation to reflect on what it really means to be a parent, or to be the parent that your child deserves. The mentor, who knows in their heart what is right for their own child.

I am not a psychologist and I do not pretend to be one. I am simply a parent who would like to share a different perspective, or my point of view, with all new parents or parents-to-be. I have not always seen things from this angle, but becoming a mother made me realise how wonderful and powerful we all are, and have always been from the day we were born.

We are extraordinary, we are amazing beings with so much potential. But then as we grow up, we are taught that we need to behave a certain way, that we need to become someone in order to be taken into consideration.

The ideas of competition and conflict have been programmed into us so deeply that we wear different layers of social consciousness and behave according to what is socially acceptable, that we forget who we really are.

In fact, if we ever asked ourselves who we are, we would realise the answer to that question is the result of our education: it is what we have been taught to believe and accept about ourselves.

The stories we tell ourselves have great power over us.
Depending on how they are told, our stories can enlighten
or mislead, inspire or discourage.

- Mike Bellah -

The way we see life, our persona, has been created by the way we were brought up, the life we saw our parents living, and the experiences we had growing up. No matter how much we appreciate certain ways of living and believe in how good they are, we justify our incapacity to change by blaming our past experiences, and we just accept that this is how we are and we cannot change.

We are worth changing the way we think. It is hard work, but that work is love made visible.

I believe that we can all change, however often we need a reason to change. For me, becoming a mum made me a better person. In fact, I believe becoming a parent enlightens us. It motivates us to change, to be open to new teachings and to look for ways to raise our children that are different from how we were brought up. This is because, deep down we know that how we were raised was not entirely right for us. We know this because we realise that we have never been completely ourselves and lived to our fullest potential.

For me, parenting is a fascinating and rather wonderful experience. It has been a journey of growth and self-discovery. Every day I discover new feelings, new strengths and weaknesses, and I gain more knowledge. Each day I am surprised at how much can be learned by simply observing our children. Parenting truly means growing alongside these little persons.

No one can ever prepare us to be parents. There are no exams we can take so that when we become parents, we already know what to do. This is why we want to learn how to be perfect parents and raise perfect children so much that parenting becomes a must-do job instead of a loving experience.

And when parenting becomes a job, we start to focus on the results of what we want to achieve. It is not about the children anymore; it is what we want from them.

We want our children to be "good" children, which for them often is translated as "quiet "or not a trouble for us grown-ups. The main reason why our children may feel this way is because in this busy life we use fear and reward as instruments to control behaviour.

I realised how wrong this was for me one day, when I asked my five-year-old daughter to eat her dinner and she replied: "If you want me to eat, I will only do it if I watch the iPad while eating."

We may think that rewards are the perfect incentives for children and that they will motivate them to be well-behaved. In the short term rewards probably work, but I do not think that they do in the long term. In my opinion, we shouldn't be using rewards to control behaviour, instead we should be rewarding the effort.

Parenting should not be about control.

It is true that parents need to be in control, in charge. As parents, it is our responsibility to create a safe and healthy environment for our children. But being in control does not mean controlling children, making them do whatever we want them to do. And if they do as we ask and become what we want them to become, what is the cost?

Is it worth it if our children lose themselves?

I started asking myself how we can know for sure what is right and wrong. On what do we base our conclusions? I thought of all the pieces of advice I received from the moment I became a mother, and I realised how different they all were, and still are. I know that it all came with the right intention; but it did not come from the right place - the heart. It came from everyone's mind and beliefs about the way the things should be, and was based on everyone's own experiences. I am not saying that their beliefs are right, wrong, good or bad; I just believe they are not enough if we want to raise happy children.

I believed that becoming a parent was a kind of completion of a life cycle. It was as if by now we should have mastered what it means to be children, what children want, and how a teenager feels when he or she is not understood. It felt as if we should simply be ready to be parents. But it is not and most of the time we forget what it was like to be a child, and only remember what is like to be an adult, and what is expected from a responsible adult.

As parents, we are aware of the role we play in programming our children's beliefs and the impact they have on our children's lives. We all know that when it comes to education (apart from the academic one), parenting is fundamental. Parenting is where our young people's life education begins: they learn from us before they are exposed to a formal education with other children their age. Children observe their environment very carefully. They memorise the worldly wisdom they hear from their parents, and as result their parents' behaviour and beliefs become their own.

We know how important it is to be aware of our own behaviour, and most importantly the language to use with our children. Children learn in the first 7/9 years of life by observation - by observing us. How we solve problems, how we confront something hurtful that has happened to us and more. The most important thing is, how do we model? Actions are as important as our language.

We think that just telling children how they should behave is enough for them to learn, but it is not. We need to model the behaviour we want to see in them.

Parenting is not about us and our expectations. It is about our children; it is about paying attention to them, to their feelings and their thoughts. We cannot possibly expect them to act like little adults if we are not even close to treating them as if they are. When we start teaching them right from wrong, we unconsciously deprive them of their innocence and their purity, and we limit their expression, imagination and creativity. We teach them fear, judgment of best and worst, competitiveness, jealousy and possessiveness, when they have yet to experience all of these.

We bring to this soul lifting and formidable experience the baggage of society's rules, which blur the way we see our children and prevent us from seeing them as they really are - just children with the wonder to learn, the need to be encouraged, cared for, cherished, and above all, to be loved. They are worthy of our unconditional love; not the conditional love that we are so used to as a reward for good behaviour, but true unconditional love.

Are we parents capable of loving our children unconditionally? Are we able to break the mould of our minds, to change the way we view life, and especially how we see our children?

I would like this little booklet to be considered an invitation to reflect. As you read through the pages you will find at the end of some paragraphs questions which I do not necessarily answer. The main reason is because I would like you to answer and reflect on those questions.

The aim of this book is to help parents re-think parenting and invite them to create their own unique parenting path, based on what they feel and not on what they think is right.

We should make sure our teachings come from the right source and I believe that is our heart.

*It is not the child who is taught love,
but the child who has experienced
love that grows into a healthy,
happy, well-adjusted adult.*

- Maxwell Maltz, Psycho Cybernetics -

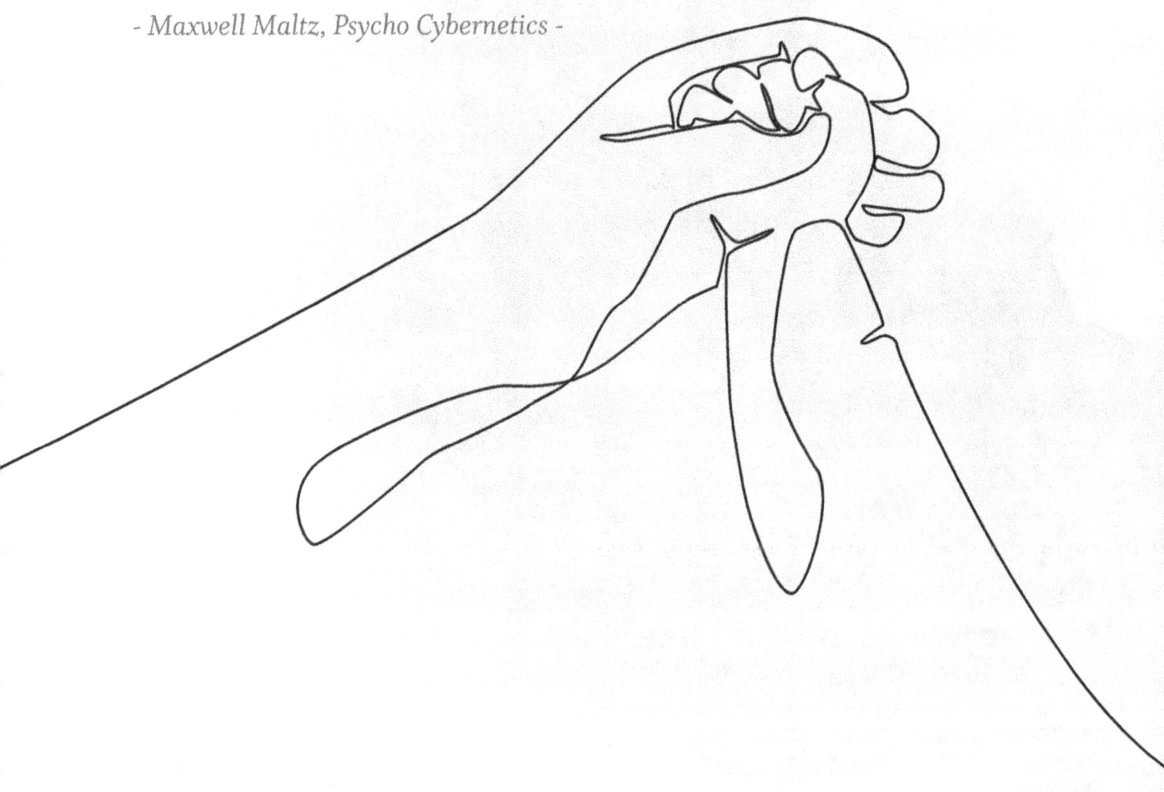

Unconditional Love

There is no doubt that we all love our children. We know that, and probably our children know that too, but how do they perceive the love they receive from us?

We want our children to be confident, resilient, responsible, independent, kind, generous, and above all happy. These are amazing qualities, but have we ever taken the time to think about how we can achieve them ourselves, or raise children with them?

Have we ever taken the time to check if our behaviour is consistent with what we want our children to be?

Are we too busy putting them to bed, getting them ready in the morning, making sure they go to school on time, they do their homework, that we forget to actually pay attention to them?

I believe we are too busy. We never stop, and life has become a race.

And because of the way we see this frenetic life we often mistake happiness for security, and we start focusing on achievements instead of on each child as a person.

Most of the time, we want our children to be well behaved because that is what we want to hear about them from other parents.

Being a parent can easily become a competition for what we require from our children. We do not stop to ask about their feelings, or even our feelings, but we concentrate on the result.

We tell them what to do and how to do it, we tell them how to behave, and we reward them every time we get what we want from them. We are so focused on ensuring that they internalize our values that we don't help them develop their own.

> ### And this, to me, is the opposite of wanting our kids to become independent thinkers.

It seems we have forgotten the main goal, which is to love our children.

We withdraw our children's affection as a form of discipline, forgetting that in doing so we are teaching them that our love turns on and off according to their behaviour. Instead we need to make sure that, as Alfie Kohn says, our "I love you" is never perceived by them as "do as I say"

Our children's life should not be a fight to gain our approval. We should love them for no good reason. And it is important that they know they are loved. Every single moment we spend with them, the way we communicate with them, pay attention to them, respect them, and treat them should be a demonstration of pure love.

Loving children unconditionally means understanding their developmental stage and address their misbehaviour accordingly. We should respect their wonder and desire to explore and learn. We should never punish them for being children. Punishment never works, because if it did, we would not have to keep using it over and over again.

Our children need and love us more than they can ever say and, in this journey called life, they can often become confused by feeling judged and unloved. This makes them look outside of themselves for answers, reasons, or paths to follow. This is where unconditional love can give its best, and teach them that they do not need a reason to live for, and they do not need to search for one; THEY are the reason. They do not need to give a meaning to their life; THEY are the meaning of their life. We need to teach children to never look outside themselves for meaning, because while they do, they will not see how amazing they are, or be truly free.

If a child really needs a reason to live, then let that reason be the only thing that will always be with them - love of self.

Teach them that life is a beautiful stage on which they can freely express their creativity, their beauty, and their sublime being for the only reason there is: to be happy.

They are worthy of being loved for who they are. Loving this way transcends social consciousness, rises above acceptance and transcends judgement.

This is the love we need to teach our children. This is the love they need to feel from us, and this is the love they need to feel for themselves.

There is no greater purpose in life than to live for the fulfilment of the self and do the things that bring joy and happiness. This is unconditional love.

Of all the life skills available to us, communication is perhaps the most empowering.

- Brett Morrison -

Communication

Just like all mothers, I have an amazing bond with my little one. Every time I look into her eyes, I see the love light that she is and I'm filled with so much love that there are no words to describe it. In those moments I am reminded of how important our relationship is, and how important she is to me. However, I know it can be challenging to nourish this bond in everyday life. We know it is there but often we take it for granted and as we start to focus on our children's future, what we want them to become, we start to lose that initial bond. As we concentrate on the behaviour, we see only the external and neglect what is actually happening inside.

Communication plays a very important role in building a healthy relationship with children, particularly when they are very young and we are helping them to express their feelings and their thoughts.

Most of the time we associate the word "communication" with talking, but that is not what it actually is. Communication is also listening.

Taking time to listen to our children also gives us time to choose the right words and the appropriate tone of voice when responding to them.

And the way we communicate with our children determines the way they respond to us.

Communication should
never be a tool for
controlling an outcome,
but a tool to connect.

How we deal with what we consider issues or mistakes, is very important in helping us to better understand the motives behind them, and to better know our children.

We are their anchor, their safe place. They should feel safe to come and talk to us without the fear of being punished or judged. They need to feel free to safely express their feelings. Misbehaviour or hysterical crying and yelling are often considered to be a cry for attention, but I think they are a call for help. As frustrating as this kind of situation feels - and I know how much it can – we need to acknowledge the need they have to be listened to and taken into consideration. Children, particularly when they are very young, don't know how to verbalise their feelings, and often tantrums are the only way they can communicate.

We should not take their misbehaviour, or as some would say 'button-pushing behaviour', personally.

It takes time and requires patience to physically bring ourselves to a child's level and talk to them while looking them in the eye; but it takes no effort, no thought and very little time to keep them quiet by giving them something or by punishing with time out. I know most parents do not consider time out as punishment, but to me it is because it is forced and is not willingly agreed to by the child.

It is very easy to make children fearful by using punishment when they repeat undesirable behaviour, but have we actually taught them anything? Have they learned anything? Most importantly, have we, the parents, learned the reason behind that behaviour? Have we discovered the cause and realised how to deal with it? With punishment, all we have done is to correct the problem by making the child take the consequences of their actions. They have not been taught to take responsibility for their own actions; instead that responsibility has been taken away from them. They certainly have not been taught problem solving.

We sometimes need to just stop and ask ourselves: are we adding love to a conversation, are we building our children up, are we connecting with them? Because punishment is far from connection; it is disconnection.

I understand most of the parents talk about discipline and how children need to be disciplined, but what does that mean? What is discipline? Often it is associated with punishment, but that is not it.

I personally prefer not to use this word, but if I ever had to give it a meaning, I would say it is our attitude when we provide our children with care, love and the guidance they will depend on.

**Remind your children
about their courage,
their strength, resilience,
and how much light they
bring into your life.**

Make them feel they are safe with you and that your love is greater than any mistake they can ever make.

Speak to your children as if they are the wisest, kindest, most beautiful and magical humans on earth, for what they believe they will become.

\- Brooke Hampton -

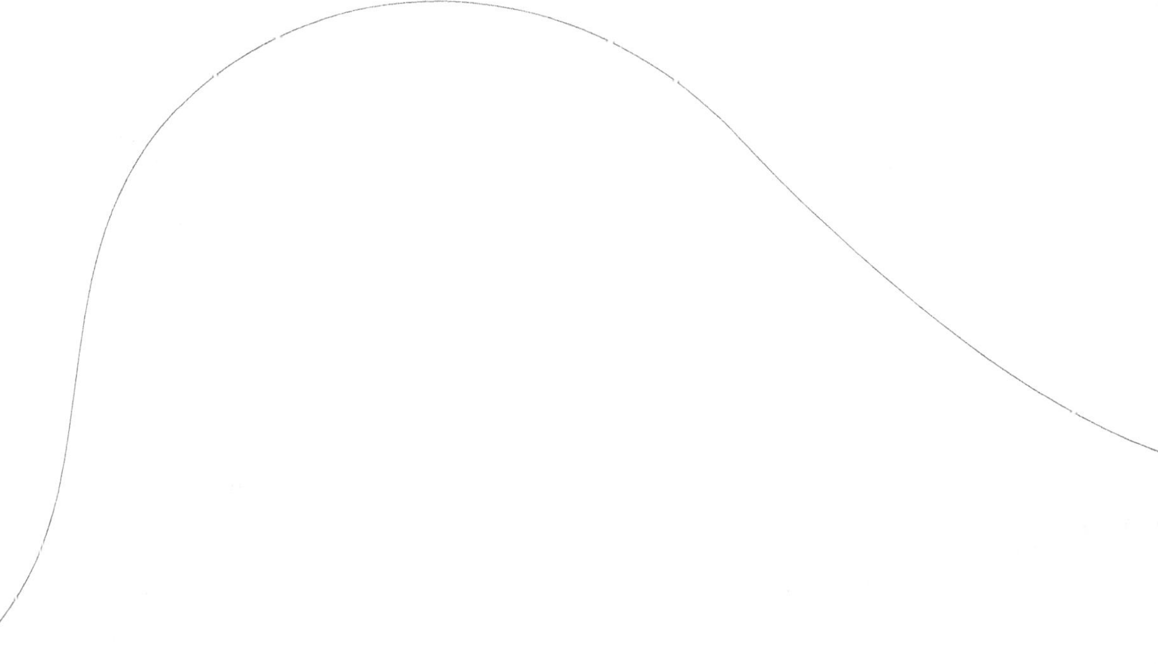

A person's a person
no matter how small.

- Dr Seuss -

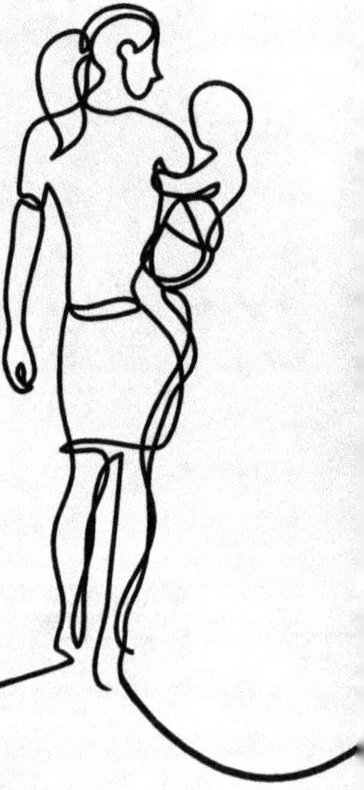

Respect

Respect is something we feel entitled to receive. I was raised in a family where the elderly people are entitled to respect because of their age, powerful people are entitled to respect because of what they have achieved, and parents are entitled to respect because they are the parents. This is the socially acceptable way of looking at respect, and it is common. And I am not saying it is wrong, I just find it incomplete. And I ask myself, what about the children? When do they get to be respected? How long does a child have to wait before it is socially acceptable for them to receive respect? I believe that a child does not have to wait, because entitlement to respect cannot be just related to age, actions or position.

Respect to me is not an entitlement.

Respect is a fundamental human right. We have this right from the moment we come to this life. When it comes to children, from the moment they begin their life we should respect them. We should respect their bodies and respect their space, and we should respect them as human beings. They are people in their own right, with wants and desires, just as we adults are.

And the thing is, we do not need to teach them what respect is; children don't come into this world being disrespectful - they are taught disrespect by observing our behaviour.

We do not need to teach
children anything; we
need to be everything we
want to teach them.

We all need to be responsible, respectful and loving people.

Respecting children means letting them be who they are, letting them experience life, and giving them permission to be human, just like us.

Modelling respect is loving and caring for everything around us, and everyone with whom we come into contact.

Respect is the absence of humiliation and shaming. This all means speaking to children with the regard they deserve, taking the time to choose the words we say to them. Reflect on the meaning that each word holds, and on how powerful each word is.

I know it is not easy to maintain that respect through times of challenging behaviour, or after a very exhausting day. The reality is, our children probably had a busy and tiring day at school or childcare, just like us.

We need to acknowledge that. We are the adults, and we are the models.

We should always remind ourselves that the way we treat our children gives them permission to treat others - including us - the same way.

When awareness is brought to an emotion,
power is brought to your life.

- Tara Meyer Robson -

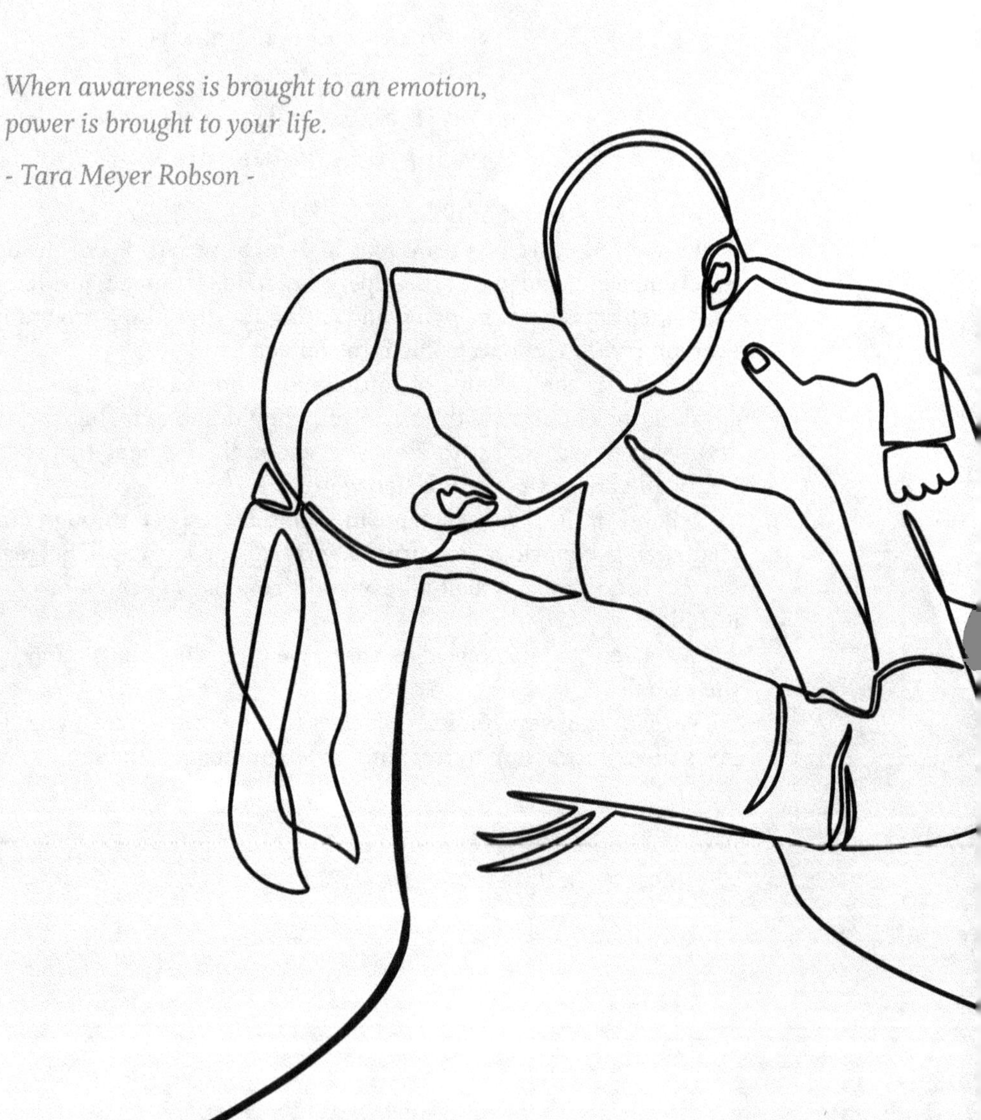

Emotional Intelligence

Emotional intelligence: I really love these two words together. They give parents the opportunity to once again demonstrate love for these little people who trust them. This is where we get to help our children to recognise and identify their emotions. Emotional intelligence is being aware and intelligent about our own emotions. To be aware of our emotions means knowing and understanding them; and being intelligent is about the way we use them in our everyday life.

It is essential to recognise the rightful place of each emotion.

We live in a society where it is often not considered a compliment to be thought of as emotional, yet it is a compliment say someone is intelligent. We live in a world that disregards feelings because they are thought to be less important than reason, and irresponsible, childish and full of nonsense.

We live in a society that teaches us to deny our feelings, to ignore or even to control them.

Emotional intelligence brings together these two aspects of humanness. We should welcome all emotions, every single of them. Children need freedom to express their deepest, oddest and even, what my seem to us, inappropriate feelings. We cannot control our children's feelings, but what we can control is the freedom they feel to express them.

Often when we see our children in pain, even from something as simple as a scratch on their knee, we tend to dismiss and diminish their feelings by using words like "get over it, it is nothing". We should not invalidate their response to a situation just because we view it as an overreaction. No matter how nonsensical their point of view might seem to us, our children need our understanding. Acknowledging their feelings provides them with the feeling of being understood.

**We ask children to hide
their emotions just for
tiny things;**

what will happen when they grow up and have bigger issues than a scratch on the knee?

It is our job to help them understand the reasons why they are feeling that way, so that they learn how to deal with their emotions. Hiding or ignoring the feelings will not make our children grow stronger because eventually these unresolved feelings will come to the surface, and sooner or later they will have to face them.

Children need to know that feelings matter, that they have the power to change us. And they need to be able to know and understand feelings, just as feelings seem to understand us better than we actually understand ourselves.

*If you are tuned out of your own emotions,
you will be poor at reading them in other people.*

- Daniel Goleman -

Perfection

I have always believed that perfection is an illusion.

Just like physical beauty, perfection is also relative. Each and every one of us has our own standards of perfection and beauty, based on the way we see things. The way we see things is based on our perception; the way we perceive things depends on the way we think; the way we think depends on who we are; and who we are is based on our experiences. We carry a lot of emotional baggage with us. We are not completely free from our past, our parent's teachings, and our society. We have been programmed psychologically and neurologically from the time we were born, so that how we experience life, interpret reality and react does not come from freedom, but from patterns, old experiences and wounds.

Therefore, if perfection is an illusion, it does not exist. And most people would agree with that, but for some reason we keep looking for it – we want the perfect partner, the perfect child, the perfect parent. And we behave according to the need to be perfect, to be better than anybody else, and we ask that from our children too. But our children need to know that they don't have to be "perfect". We need to teach them that

**life is a journey
of learning and
exploring, and not a
finished product.**

As Barbara De Angelis says in her book The Choice For Love: "Our children need to know that they will do stupid things, they will be blind, that probably they will not be able to live to their expectations and that all this is ok, because this is what means to be human, this is the human condition".

> Teach your children that
> there are no bad or good
> decisions in life, but only
> decisions from which
> they can gain experience,
> knowledge and wisdom.

Teach them that not doing something for fear of failure is already a failure – and more than that, it is a failure from which nothing is learned.

Parents, in every moment give your children the opportunity and the freedom to express joy, show kindness, be happy and be themselves.

Joy is the freedom of being without fear and guilt; it is the freedom of expression without judgement. This is how all children should feel, and how they should see life.

Let it be your joy to watch them grow and evolve, experiencing life without expectations.

There is a very strong connection between expectations and disappointment – a word that parents so often use inappropriately. We should never use the word "disappointment" with our children. Disappointment comes from expectations, and the truth is we should not expect anything from anyone, not even from ourselves.

> Don't live your life
> according to what you
> think you should be
> receiving or what you
> think you deserve.

The way we perceive things comes from a long life of "good" or "bad" experiences, as judged by ourselves; and they have formed the filter through which we see and interpret things. In having expectations, we take for granted that everything around us, including people, does not change.

And when it comes to children, how could they ever disappoint us? They are learning from us. So what are we really disappointed in?

Looking at perfection and disappointment this way helped me to cease feeling guilt, placing blame on others and judging others. I accept that everyone is trying to live the best they can with the information they have at any given time. This opens the door to forgiveness, which is often thought of as a gift to others, but is really a gift to ourselves. With forgiveness, you can liberate yourself from the bitterness that comes from disappointment. It is only our attitudes and our judgements that determine the experience we have in our life.

> Teach children to
> embrace life. They are
> worthy of this life's
> adventures.

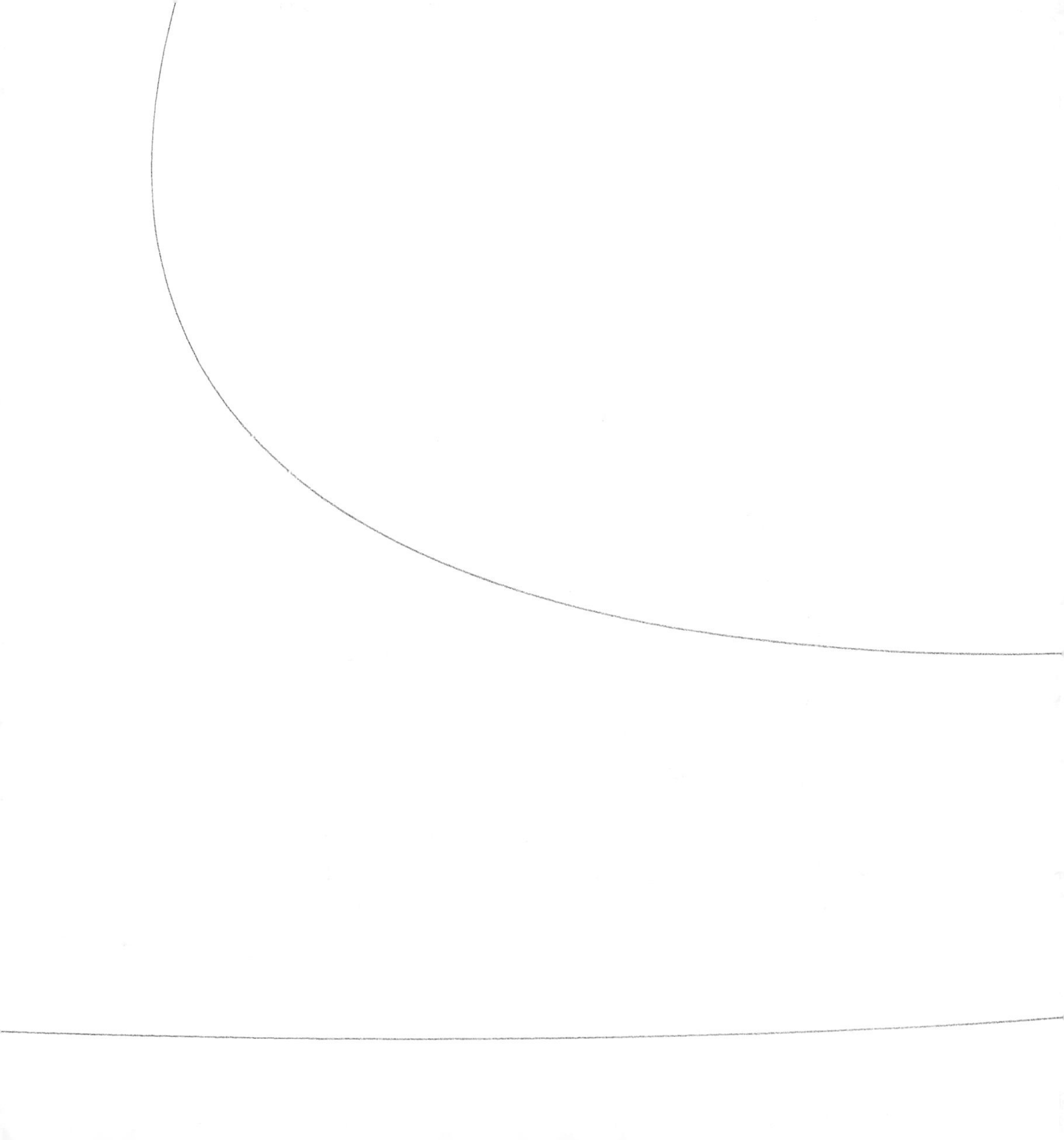

To esteem your self is to
recognise your power.

- Caroline Myss -

Healthy
Self-Esteem

If we looked up what self-esteem means, we would find it is an individual's subjective evaluation of their own worth. It is the positive or negative evaluation of the self, as in how we feel about it.

Self-esteem encompasses the beliefs about oneself (for example "I'm unloved", "I'm unworthy"), as well as emotional states, such as pride and shame.

This definition of self-esteem somehow involves other people's approval and acceptance, but that is not a healthy self-esteem. A healthy self-esteem liberates you from that need and helps you to break away from the fear of being humiliated. With a healthy self-esteem, you can rely on your own integrity and values remaining unshakeable no matter what circumstances you are in.

I believe self-esteem is the most important element in creating a healthy relationship, not only with others but with ourselves.

I always associated it with self-confidence, with the power we hold in a relationship, or the power given by a position we hold in society. All this power that have according to the means we possess, builds our confidence and contributes to our sense of worthiness; but it is actually quite superficial, because the moment you lose the power, all the rest is gone. So healthy self-esteem does not derive from the power we hold, but from understanding how powerful we are.

It is hard to understand the power we hold, when life has no significance. All that we teach our children is: to strive to be better than, to have more than, that life is a battle where the big shark eats the little shark. And this is how life loses its worthiness in our children's eyes. Everything that has to do with humanness, vulnerability, and sensitivity is seen as a weakness, as unworthiness, but actually it is quite the opposite.

Being vulnerable and feeling the pain that others inflict on us makes us understand how powerful we are. In feeling pain when someone hurts us with one word or the sadness when loved ones do not pay attention to us, we realise how powerful we are. That is the moment when we understand the importance of every word we choose and every thought we have, our capacity to either destroy or help another person, and the destructive or constructive power we have.

So the question is:

Do we esteem ourselves enough to empower our children?

Children look up at us and wonder what we think of them. Seeking the approval of their parents is taught to them, just as it was taught to us. The sense of our accountability is important, but it is even more crucial that when teaching our children to be themselves, we stop using comparisons. When raising our children, we stop worrying what people would think or would say about us. If we raise our children based on what is expected of "perfect" or successful parents, on the fear of being judged as "bad" or "good" parents, we are teaching our children to make choices out of fear of what we, the parents, might think of them.

If we were to realise how many of our decisions about our children's education are based on other people's approval, we might see how easily we have given away our power. This is because our way of educating our children is often driven by what is expected by us. We need to be true to ourselves, and to do what we feel is right for us without questioning what others would say.

> **A parent's fear of being judged should not be greater than their love for their child.**

Healthy self-esteem is going beyond our beliefs, the values which have created our personality, and our personal truth. Going beyond all of these gives us the opportunity to look at things from a different perspective and helps us to pay attention to our own behaviour, the way we treat others, and the way we interpret the words of others.

When we have self-esteem to the point that we trust ourselves, we raise our children form the heart. In doing so, we pay attention what we say to our children and we recognise their power. We do not make comparisons and judge, which can create self-doubt and limited self-belief; and we do not want our children to be fearful or to make decisions based on fear, but out of wonder and curiosity.

If children base their decisions on the fear of failing, or of being judged or humiliated, they will never know their own capability and their full potential.

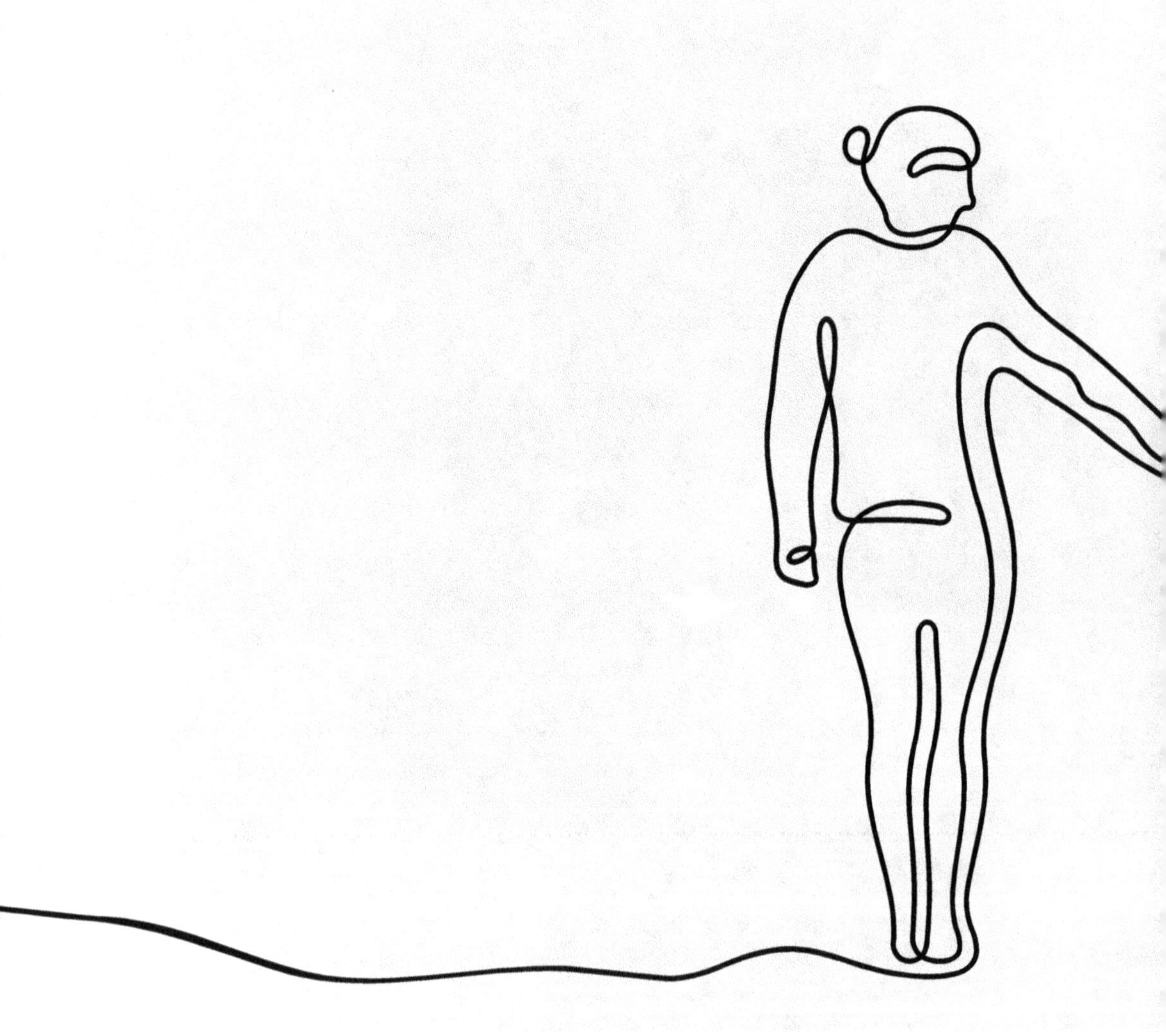

Consideration

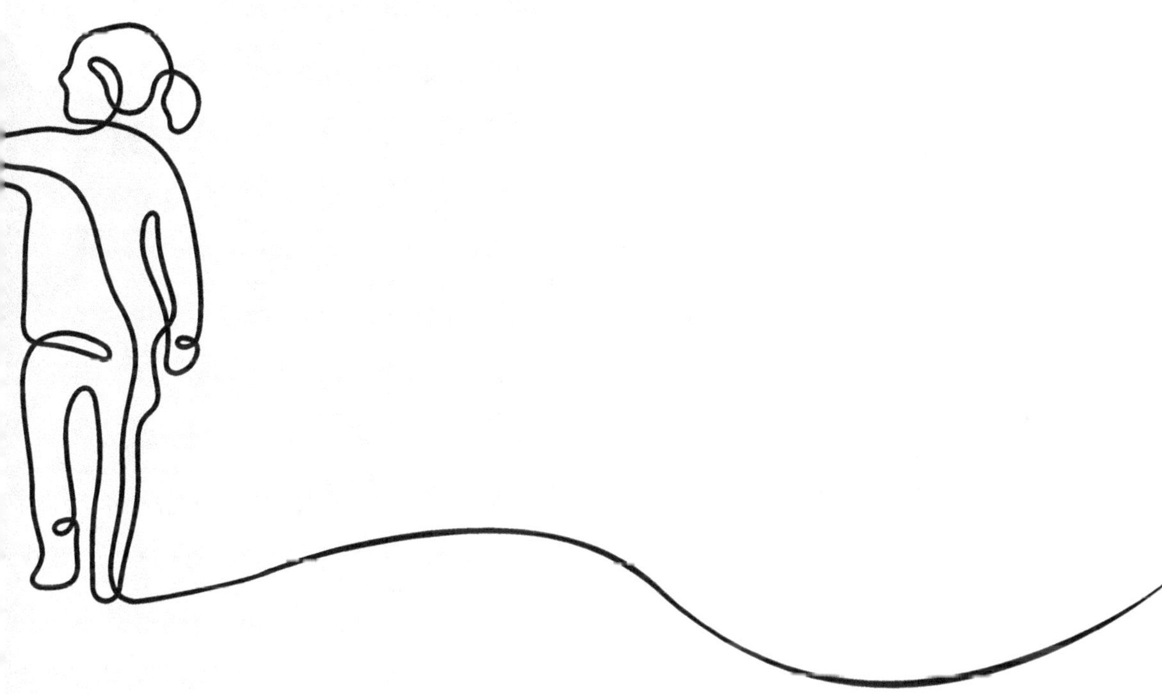

In my opinion there are no bad kids and no kids are bullies, but there are unhappy kids. Today's parents see life as a very competitive and difficult race where they need to give the best, without being distracted. Therefore, rewarding children in order to make them well-behaved, has become a priority in order to keep them quiet. And we think we have it under control, but we don't. Yes, rewards and punishments work very well in the short term, but what about when our children are not children anymore?

When children grow and no longer listen and do as we ask them to, parents think they have changed; but the truth is they haven't. They still do what they have been taught to do or asked to do, they are just not listening to us parents anymore. They are listening to someone else - their peers. They are still behaving exactly the way we have taught them to. In fact, some of them will remain the good listeners they have always been, who will always follow instructions based upon promises or threats. And some will become their parents - who will punish or make promises in order to get something.

We have created victims and bullies, and then surprised, we wonder what happened to society and to schools.

There is no one to blame but us, we are depriving our children of their parent's love. We are so focused on providing for them materially that we forget that we are the people these little humans are looking up to and learning from every day. Subconsciously or consciously we are teaching them how hard life is and how hard we need to work to build a future for them, a future that for some reason is being pushed even further away and seems to never arrive.

This does not mean we don't have to work or provide for our children. This means we need any reason to find a balance. It is our responsibility to take care of our children, look after them, and guide them to adulthood, but we need to do that in an honest, loving and compassionate way which they deserve. In order to do so, we need to change the way we think about life, about what it means to be human, what is means to be a parent.

I would like to invite you to ask yourself the following simple question: are you giving your child the best version of you?

We all try to do what is best for our kids, or what we think is best. But if we ever have to justify the way we talk to our children or how we treat them, in order to convince ourselves that we are doing the right thing, the answer to question is no, we are not giving the best version of ourselves to our child.

The only reason we would try to convince ourselves that it is, would be because it doesn't feel right inside us. It doesn't feel right in our heart, and we are trying to gather all the information we have in our mind to shut down that feeling. But we should not do that, because our children need the best of us.

Let us raise children who do not need to fight against themselves, or to hide who they are. Let's make sure our children have a childhood that they don't need to recover from.

Be bold and courageous enough to empower your children. Be bold and courageous enough to choose love. Be bold and courageous enough to claim yourself.

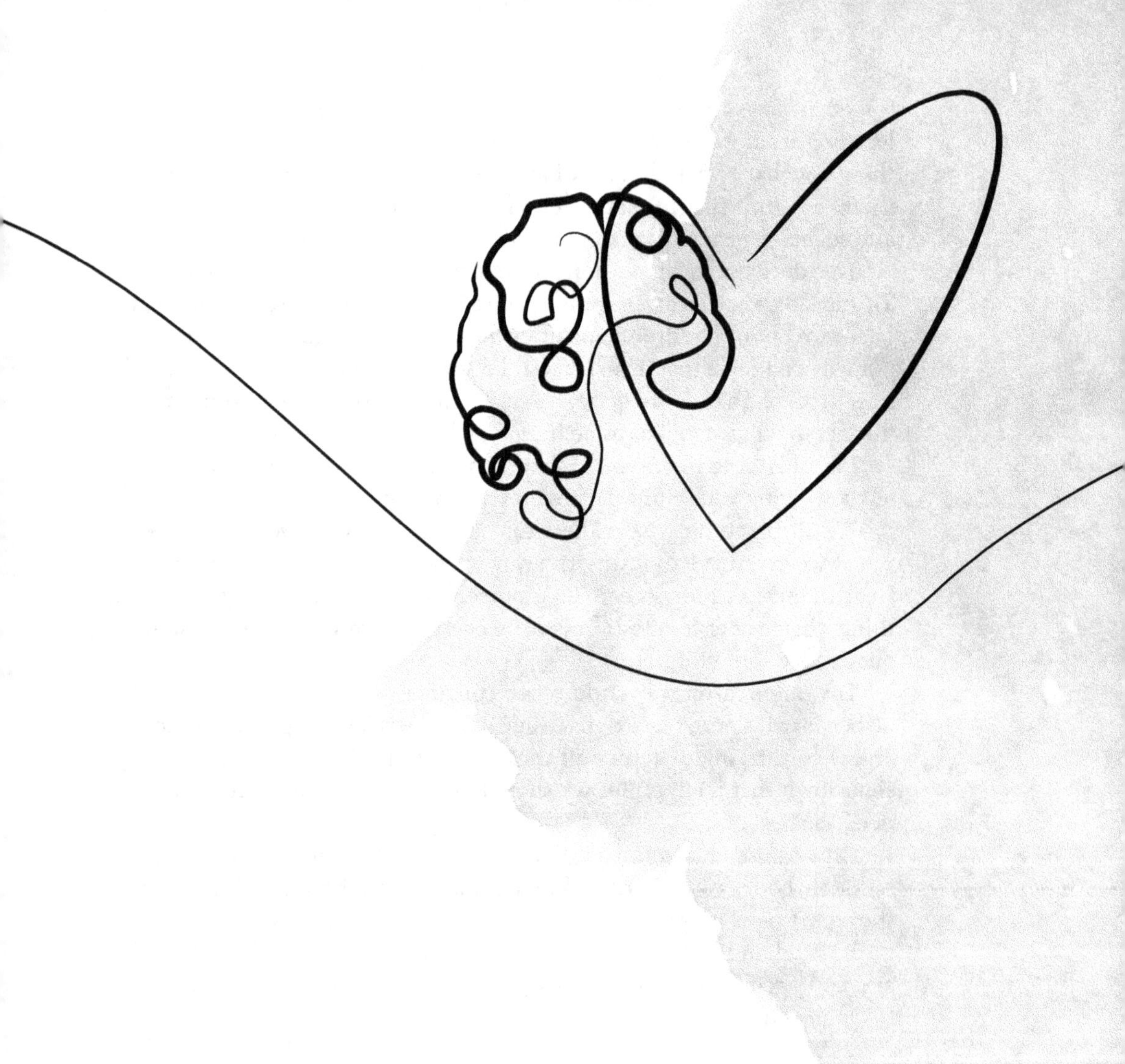

To My Daughter

I truly understood what love is the very first
moment I held you in my arms.

You made my heart sing by just being you.

Watching you crawling around the house and
then walking your first steps and growing every
day is pure happiness.

When I see you smile, my heart smiles. When I
see you laugh, my heart laughs.

It does not wonder who made you smile and
laugh because it doesn't matter.

You being happy matters.

Thanks to you, my beloved daughter, things that
were unnoticeable to me made sense when they
brought laughter to you.

I will encourage you to be yourself and I will
support you in your choices.

I will remind you how extraordinary you are and
how much courage you have.

I will help you follow your bliss, and encourage
you to do what makes you feel most alive.

I will tell you not to be afraid of making
mistakes, because no mistakes are bigger than
my love for you.

You are safe with me.

I cannot imagine a better life than this one in
which I watch you change, evolve and grow.

I love you

Thank you for choosing me to be your mum.

Bibliography

Books

Barbara De Angelis, *The Choice for Love: Entering into a New, Enlightened Relationship with Yourself, Others and the World*, 2017.

Dr Joe Dispenza, *Breaking the Habit of Being Yourself: How to Lose Your Mind and Create a New One*, 2012.

Dr Joe Dispenza, *Evolve Your Brain: The science of Changing Your Mind*, 2007.

Carol S Dweck PhD, *Mindset: The New Psychology of Success. How we can learn to fulfil our full potential*, 2007.

Bruce H Lipton PhD, *The Biology of Belief: Unleashing the Power of Consciousness, Matter and Miracles*, 2005.

Ramtha: The White Book, 2005.

Videos

Finding Joe. Documentary, 2011.

Caroline Myss: *Why We Search for Personal Power and Self-Esteem*. Workshop recorded at the Sofia Institute, 19-20 October 2018.